THE POWER OF THIN

How Fat Stole My Body

CARRIE LITTEN

This book is designed to provide information that the author believes to be accurate on this subject matter covered, but it is sold with the understanding that neither the author nor the publisher is offering individualized advice tailored to any specific person or experience. Please remember that I (Carrie Litten, author) am in no way a medical professional and do not pretend to be in anyway. Please always consult your medical professional on anything you do or don't do in terms of your surgery and recovery plan. Always remember that everyone's body and person is an individual and may have same or different experiences and feelings than I had. The content within this book is only my personal experiences, feelings; opinions and what worked and did not work for me personally. My friends or family experiences were my witness and perspective to their hardships not testimony or quotes on their behalf.

No warranty is made with respect to the accuracy or completeness of the information contained herein, and both the author and the publisher specifically disclaim any responsibility for any liability, loss, or risk, personal or otherwise, which is incurred a consequence, directly or indirectly, of the use and application of any of the contents of this book.

FORBZ HOUSE LLC
7371 Atlas Walk Way Suite 142
Gainesville, VA 20155

Copyright © 2014 by Carrie Litten

All rights reserved, including the right to reproduce this book or portions thereof in any form whatsoever. For information address FORBZ HOUSE LLC 7371 Atlas Walk Way Suite 142, Gainesville, VA 20155

First edition printing: 2014

For information about special discounts on bulk purchases, please contact the publisher **FORBZ HOUSE, LLC** at the above listed address. U.S. trade bookstores and wholesalers: Please contact **FORBZ HOUSE, LLC** www.forbzhouse.com

For information on this author guest speaking, live events or book signing, please contact business@thepowerofthin.com

ISBN 978-0-9863391-2-7

DEDICATION

To my mom **Sarah** who has had the same weight loss surgery that I had and has battled the weight loss struggles all her life as well.
She is the back bone in our family.
To my dad **James** who is always doing something interesting and funny and always the apple of everyone's eye!
To my sister **Cheryl** who has been one of the best fashion consultants, one of my mentors and a great cheer leader any one sister could have. Who continues to be supportive in my life today.
To my brother **Jason** who is always down to rough housing and talking about fast cars and his wife **Melissa** who loves him, puts up with his crazy projects and lets him be himself.
To my son **Brandon** who is the best computer guru I know. He was out programming me in visual basic in 11th grade and has grown up to be a great young man.
To my daughter **Kristen** who no matter what, no matter how cluttered my closet could get... she could always find that missing high heel and who has the best heart melting hugs and smile.
To my sister **Kristy** who always did the right thing and made the most perfect toll house chocolate chip cookies in the world. Every single one looked like the photos in a toll house cookie ad! May she rest in peace and always look down proud from heaven.
"**To** my friends **Tina**, **Beth** and **Everyone** who has ever battled one of the greatest challenges in my life "Obesity & Weight Loss".

CONTENTS

Acknowledgments · i

CHAPTER 1 · The Decision · 3

CHAPTER 2 · A New Beginning · 6

CHAPTER 3 · Learning to Eat Again · 10

CHAPTER 4 · What I Experienced 1st Year · 15

CHAPTER 5 · Photos Over The Years · 17

CHAPTER 6 · Wardrobe Freedom & Challenges · 21

CHAPTER 7 · Emotional & Social Challenges "Choices" · 28

CHAPTER 8 · New Experiences & Living Life · 35

CHAPTER 9 · Vitamins & Maintaining Healthy Habits · 38

CHAPTER 10 · I Still Hate Exercise · 43

ACKNOWLEDGMENTS

I would like to acknowledge my doctor
Dr. Denis J. Halmi, MD of Woodbridge, Virginia.
"The Master of His Expertise and One of The Greatest Doctors I Know!"

CHAPTER 1

The Decision

STATEMENT: *Before reading the contents in this book, please remember that I (Carrie Litten) am in no way a medical professional and do not pretend to be. Always consult your medical professional on anything you do or don't do in terms of your surgery and recovery plan. Always remember that everyone's body and person is an individual and may have same or different experiences and feelings than I have. The content within this book is only my personal experiences, feelings, opinions and what worked and did not work for me personally. My experiences described of friends or family were my witness and perspective to their hardships not testimony or quotes on their behalf.*

Years and years of struggling to lose weight and missed promotions on the job due to not fitting the visual mold. The hurt of not being socially accepted with certain groups of people due to not fitting the perfect weight mold. Diet after diet... I can go on and on with this part of my book. I will spare everyone the crying about my personal struggles before surgery. If you are reading this then you know what it feels like and know what happens at work and in society.

In 1996 my sister Kristy died of type I diabetes, many of my cousins have lost limbs due to the same reason. By 2003 I was told that I would end up with type 2 diabetes and have to go on insulin if I did not start doing something about it now. Already my quality of life was not there. I couldn't ride bikes, walk far or play in the outdoors with my small children. It was very difficult to exercise and when I did there was no change in my weight. This lead to depression based on personal appearance and self-esteem. I asked my doctor what my choices were? Medications, Diets... I wanted something permanent. I was told about the 3 types of weight loss surgery that I could choose from, possible risks, quality of life...etc.

I chose the gastric bypass surgery. There are many other choices that can be used to achieve the rapid weight loss my surgery gave me. Each one has its own set of positive and negative sides. I am not going to give my opinion on which one is better or not than the other, I feel it's a personal decision and not an easy one to make.

My focus for this book is to provide some insight for the reader on my personal experiences, what I went through and what I have learned through the 10 years post-gastric bypass. Not to judge or debate the types of surgeries available.

THE POWER OF THIN

CHAPTER 2

A New Beginning

It's June 5, 2003 and I go into the hospital to check in for my surgery. I weigh in at 310 lbs and little did I know at that moment in time how drastic my life would change.

Before this day came I went through many hoops. One of the things required was to attend nutrition classes. I do feel these are very important. It was suggested that I attend a pre and post bypass support group meeting. Looking back on my first 2 years post surgery, I would make it a priority to attend these support group meetings. As your body changes and you lose the weight it will become important to have others to talk to about these changes. Including an issue that I swore would "never" happen to me. Famous last words huh? One thing I would also warn to everyone that if your spouse, boyfriend, girlfriend, family members and friends close to you are not in support of your decision, you may be charting this new road alone in the end.

One meeting I attended the subject was (communication, support groups and relationships after the weight loss). Well a couple people stated that they were either divorced now or having major relationship challenges at that moment in time. Well I was in a long term relationship and had been living with a man who I intended on marrying. I went home and communicated what was said in the meeting to my boyfriend at that time and we both agreed it was not us. Well time goes on, surgery happens, everything is fine, he proposes at Christmas, we get married. Everything seemed to be great and life moved on and things were not fine. I was married 8 months and now I have been divorced since 2006. Now there were other things that he never talked with me about that came out in the end. But his main complaint was that he loved me with weight and he seemed not concerned about my quality of life and if I would have diabetes or major health problems at an early age.

One of the other red flags that I didn't realize was important to post weight loss surgery is that he wouldn't attend support group meetings with me. I actually didn't realize how important this is for the significant other and or family members to do with you as part of being supportive.

It is important on many levels! Below is a list of some reasons I have had to work through over the past 10 years. Keep in mind these do not always happen to all and do not come up right away.

Support and understanding of:

Type of Surgery you are having

Diet Changes (for life)

Vitamins and Healthy Habits (for life)

Physical Changes (1st and 2nd years are most important)

Emotional Changes (can be emotional changes on both sides)

Personal Growth Changes (some people come out of their shell and may speak their mind more and this comes across as changes people may not like. You may get responses such as "you used to be so sweet", "you were rude")

An example of what might be happening is… your letting someone know you don't agree and you probably didn't say anything before because of your weight and fear of social rejection or being called hurtful names. What I would say to the supportive partner or family member is that this can be just a phase. This person can go through a self discovery process of who they are or finally be the person they are and felt they couldn't be. I can't tell you how many times I heard toward end of my first year *"Your losing too much weight, your too thin now"*. I can't tell you how much I resented and didn't want to ever speak to the person who said that to me. I was just fresh one year out of surgery and trying to get used to my new body and emotionally adjust to looking so different in the mirror and to others. It's not the time to say these things to someone just one year out. This was one of the main reasons why I stated above how important the support group meetings are for family and friends to attend with you. The meetings allow a place for understanding, support and communication of their concerns for you. They will hear and hopefully listen to the others speak of their experiences and journey.

Just remember life and relationships will always change. I personally lost friends and a husband over this surgery. But I found out who was my real friend and loved ones in the process.

CHAPTER 3

Learning to Eat Again

This was a very hard thing to learn with my stubborn hard headedness, along with the bad eating habits that had plagued me for years. Wow I don't know where to start on this subject… due to the fact I don't want to discourage someone from having the surgery. Before I go on anymore, I would like to make two statements.

> ***One:*** *Anything to the negative in this chapter concerning getting sick and throwing up is because I didn't listen to my doctor.*
>
> ***Two:*** *good or bad!! I do not and will never regret in any way having this surgery. To this day it was the best decision I ever made for my personal health and wellness.*

Now with that being said there is the good, bad and really ugly parts in learning to eat again. Your stomach is only going to hold about 4 oz of food and that is not a lot compared to what you could eat before. Along with the fact that the opening hole to your 4 oz stomach is smaller than what used to be. There are some things to this day I cannot eat at all and these things vary from person to person, surgery to surgery. What is my situation is just what happened to me. You may be able to eat something I cannot. To this day I will throw up for 3 to 4 hours on tuna fish, chicken, pork chops, and rice.

I feel the most important thing is to follow your doctors suggestions and always consult a professional on diet changes or problems with eating things outside your recovery plan.

I can only tell you what has worked for me in keeping the weight off all these years. And no its not throwing up all these years. Haha That was mostly the first year because I kept trying to eat things I wasn't supposed to early on in the recovery and weight loss process.

The core things I stay away from today are the same things I was told I had to give up if I wanted to be successful at keeping the weight off in the future and for life. Below is a short list of the main things I do not drink or eat anymore. This list is not a complete list and your doctor will give you information on this as part of your recovery and weight loss.

Things I stay away from:

> **All Carbonated Drinks** *(it is not whether its diet or not? it's the carbonation that can re-stretch out your stomach)*
>
> **Bread or Breaded Food**
>
> **Highly Greasy and Fast Food**
>
> **High Sugar Foods** *(Cake, Ice Cream, Candy…etc)*
>
> **Challenging Food Still** *(I Continually get Sick from.. Rice, Tuna and Chicken are the big ones for me)*

This is just part of what still affects me today and what I still don't eat. Yes.. I have been told by some family and friends *"you should be able to eat this or that by now"*. I do not feed into these comments from others. The only person who pays for listening to them and eating the food which will ultimately make me sick is me. So I just reply *"It's just the way it is and I am not going to eat something that will make me sick!"* I have had a couple times a person press on with saying to me *"That is just not normal"*. I immediately say and in a firm tone *"my stomach is not normal anymore"* and I will suggest or select something I can eat and ask them to end this conversation. It's rare but just be prepared for some people out there who will react this way or say these or something similar to you.

Do not be afraid to stand up for yourself and your stomach. Some things that can happen to you if you are not careful is: tearing open your stomach lining and then you will be back in surgery to repair what the doctor has done. You could get what they call dumping syndrome. It is very important to eat the new diet that your medical professional has set up for you to follow.

As far as going out to dinner? I very rarely have a problem finding something on a menu that I can eat. Now in the beginning, the first two years and especially the first year it's going to be very hard to eat out. The first three months I was on very soft food and liquids. Take things slow and at your own pace. Don't push yourself to keep up with an eating schedule. If something doesn't go down right or you get sick just don't push yourself to eat it again for a while. Listen to stomach and your body.

I probably stayed on soft foods longer than my doctor said I had to because I didn't like getting sick and I also was afraid of tearing the surgery that was performed. I did have two friends who had a much harder time recovering because they pushed themselves hard to eat *"like they did before surgery"* again. I would just say to them *"but your stomach isn't the same anymore and why are you trying to eat like you used to"*. One of my girlfriends ended back in emergency surgery over it. I decided right then when my girlfriend went back into the hospital that I would listen to my stomach, listen to my body and go at my own pace from that day forward.

CHAPTER 4

What I Experienced 1st Year

The 1st year was a year so full of change, happiness, excitement, learning, and growing. The first six months was eating soft foods and liquids that were healthy for me and just focusing on losing weight.

It was also learning to eat healthy and correctly, not just to lose the weight but also to reprogram a more healthy mindset moving forward. Choosing what I eat and being conscious of what I put in my mouth.

After I was released by my doctor to join a gym and start exercising around the six month mark. I decided that I would just power walk and still focus on losing all the weight within the first year then I would start building muscle with weight lifting.

Unbeknownst to me during this time of happiness of losing weight, I was unaware of the new attention I was getting from other men and how upset my soon to be husband was getting over this. Even my girlfriends noticed this and I would ask them *"what are you talking about?"* This is in another chapter but for the first three years after surgery I would look in the mirror and still see 310 lbs. There are still days I wake up to day and see that person in the mirror.

I think it is why I am still modest about how I look and always treat people over weight or not with the same respect that i had always hoped people would treat me at 300 lbs. That didn't happen many more times than none. People will always be people but I will not be that way to others ever. It is very enlightening when you can truly experience both sides.

CHAPTER 5

Photos Over The Years

Before Surgery

Before Surgery

After Surgery

THE POWER OF THIN

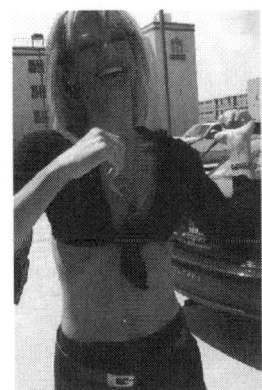

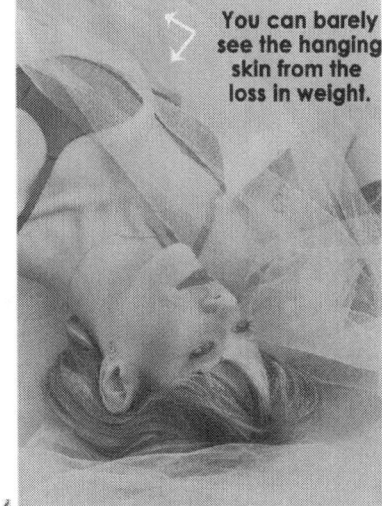

You can barely see the hanging skin from the loss in weight.

CARRIE LITTEN

THE POWER OF THIN

CARRIE LITTEN

THE POWER OF THIN

CARRIE LITTEN

CHAPTER 6

Wardrobe Freedom & Challenges

Wardrobe changes were a double edged sword in my experiences over the years. There were moments of happiness and freedom and then challenges with finding my new style and self image. I found out that it was more than just the ability to finally walk into a department store and find my size in a great style. That was just part of the learning and growing I did over the past 10 years.

Okay... to go from a size 26 to a size 5 in one year is not easy on a poor girls wallet with regards to buying new clothes as I lost weight during those 12 months. I quickly learned the weight was coming off so fast and I still had to maintain a professional look for an office job at the same time. So these few places listed below became my best friend for professional looks as I down sized. Not only cheap clothing but as you down size you can re-donate back to them.

Stores & Businesses:

> *Salvation Army Stores*
>
> *Goodwill Stores*
>
> *Any Consignment Stores Locally*

These stores really helped during my first year of rapid weight loss. It was hard to go in and shop at first because I was used to shopping at the mall. I felt guilty at first because I was not a person in great need and I felt that I should be the one giving to them not buying from them. I do donate to them now more than ever and support the great things these organizations do for so many people. I also found that there was a great supply of professional clothing in great condition. Do not feel guilty or bad for shopping there even if you make great money and can afford to shop for new sizes every month. Please re-donate back to them when you out grow a size.

After I lost the weight I had to re-learn and grow in an area you usually go through when you are a teenager. Suddenly aware of my new body, feeling truly sexy and getting new attention from men who would have never paid attention to me before. Fitting into very beautiful sexy dresses and wearing high heels. Feeling so beautiful and sexy. It was an amazing feeling that I have never to this day gotten used to.

What I had to learn was to not dress too provocative. But for a short time I did want to wear and experience what it felt like to dress in very sexy clothes and enjoy being so thin. Just remember the general public who doesn't know what you have been through will not understand and may make comments and look at you in a negative way. If you do go through this phase… just enjoy it for the moment and ignore the people who don't understand. I did tone down and work through this challenge that came with a new body.

The third thing I went through was kind of challenging and exciting at the same time. It was weird at 30 something to rediscover my new style to match my new body, new person, new attention. It can be very overwhelming, exciting and weird all at the same time. You all of a sudden have other women telling you how great you look in the dressing room and then others hating you for it. I will tell you it is exciting to start a clean slate on your own style discovery phase. I loved picking out what to wear some days… was I going to be trendy, classic, vogue?

Shopping was depressing at times and would leave the mall crying because I had a really hard time fitting my new body and either I gravitated to the plus size sections or I just didn't know where or how to start picking things out. This may seem simple to most people but it was harder to do than even I thought. I was all different sizes not just dress size, shoe size, bra and panty sizes, even a normal thing like panty hose sizes all changed. I didn't have anyone to help me with this part of my post surgery recovery.

The one thing I wish the post surgery support group had in place for me was:

- *Volunteers that would go with me shopping help in the process of fitting and sizes.*

It sometimes isn't easy to ask friends and family to do this with you. They don't really comprehend the magnitude of how emotionally hard this can be for some people. One of the best stores I found to truly help you with sizes and fitting was Victoria Secret stores. Their staff is attentive and so helpful in the fitting rooms. They are positive and are great at fitting you and getting you into the right size for your new body. I found that Dillard's Shoe department is great! They are the same with taking care of their customers. Again very positive and attentive employees who will help fit your new shoe size.

I really suggest you take the most supportive person with you when you go out to shop for the second year you are out of surgery. One main reason is all of what I stated above but also for a **"un-bias perspective"**. what I mean by "un-bias perspective" is someone who sees your new body as it truly looks to others. Because when I went shopping in my second year with a size 5 body, I would leave the store with no clothes crying because I still saw the 300 lbs in the mirror. It was a day to day… one day feeling sexy and could see my new body and then the next day seeing the 300 lbs in the mirror. Also make sure that the person going with you is "supportive" and that they truly are! Personal experiences in my past with girlfriends of mine who I had known for years would turn out to be jealous and not "supportive" in the end. They did not help in my second year of how I viewed my new body and did not aide in helping to diminish the negative visual perspective that continually plagued me when I looked in the mirror.

This may or may not go away throughout the years. Pictures, pictures, pictures… I cannot say this enough times to all of you out there who have had any type of weight loss surgery!! In hind sight I did not take enough pictures in the first two years. In my third year I did something for myself which looking back, I am so happy I did. I paid for a private professional photographer to take very sexy photos of me. I did it with lace panties, thigh highs, heels, fur wrap, gloves, pearls, pinks satin, and top less. I am not ashamed of them. It was for me and only me.

Seeing those final prints of myself did more for my self-worth and self-visual perspective of what I look like to others. I can't even begin to tell you how important that was in my growth process. It was like a small bit of closure on the person I saw in the mirror every morning. I have added a photo section in chapter 5 of this book for you all to see some of the transitions and growth over the years. *(tasteful photos)*

Again I cannot stress enough how important it is to truly find a *"real"* supportive/cheer leader for a minimum of the first 3 years of your post-surgery & recovery. Recovery is more than just the stitches and initial weight loss. That is the easy part of this whole change of life for you. Your healthy eating habits, exercise, visual perspective, emotional/mental support around you is all part of your recovery.

You see throughout this book that I will repeat myself a lot. This is because some things need to be repeated over and over.

They are points worth making in order to sink into the hard headed one's out there like myself. Things that either plagued me throughout the years or made a great impact into my emotional health and recovery process. Things I would like for you all to learn from and not have the continued heart ache, shopping depression *(in the early years)*, picking the wrong supportive persons, challenges and growth stages.

CHAPTER 7

Emotional and Social Challenges

Emotional challenges hmmm… this is a very needed chapter. My doctor focused on concerns on the subject of depression before and after surgery and for some that may be an challenge. I would like to tell about some of the things that I experienced that I didn't hear about from doctors or support group members. Some things surprised me greatly and I even at times stopped and thought… "Wow where did that come from?"

I will be honest with you and tell you right now that the first year of weight loss is a bit of an emotional roller coaster. Your just thrown back and forth with your body… rapid weight loss, plateau, rapid weight loss and plateau. Back and forth, back and forth. Plus shopping every month because your down another size.

So the first year your almost as emotional about this whole process as a pregnant woman.

The emotional and social things I would like to address that happened to me are mostly after the weight loss happened and it was more prevalent during years 2 through 5. I took me a while to work through this one. Some things were mental triggers that I really didn't know I had or would have due to all the years of obesity and then all of a sudden being thin. The following examples are my personal experiences, feelings and thoughts that ran through my mind at the time of the personal interactions with people.

These are going to be told in random order and happened during the course of my 2nd year through my 5th year post weight loss surgery.

Story One: *(trigger and very out of character for me within a public setting like this, shocked myself)* One night I was out at a local night spot, with friends, upscale place, not a violent place, dancing and really a fun place to go. Well at some point in the evening and I guess it was maybe around 12 midnight or so. I went to go use the women's bathroom, no big deal. Happy, not too much to drink *(I think this was in my 2nd year because I really was drinking water with lemon this night more than anything)* I came in, in line right behind me came in a pretty girl who was about 250-275 lbs over weight, then came in behind her was three thin and also pretty girls. I went into a stall that opened up. The obese girl went into a stall after me. The three thin girls were young and just in there touching up make up in the mirror and obviously thin all their lives I assumed by their actions/comments. The obese girl left her stall washed and left. I was finishing up, when I overheard the thin girls making fun of the obese girls weight after she left the bathroom. I don't remember all verbatim what I said but I saw black, it was like I snapped. I came out of the stall just yelling at them. Saying things like *"Your trashy bitches and have no right putting her down for the way she looks" "You need to feel fortunate you never have a weight problem nor have to deal with bitches like yourselves"*

Then one girl on her way out of the bathroom said *"Why do you care? Your thin and pretty…"* I just stopped and looked in the mirror… I was in shock of my reaction to people I didn't know at all, I was so disgusted in my own weight loss, in their hurtful words… because I was that obese girl a short time ago. How dare they think that just because I was thin it was acceptable to talk about her in front of me. I remember thinking to myself how many thin people allow others to say hurtful things and don't say anything. This was one of my major first time experiences to the fact I was accepted as thin and pretty within the eyes of *(society deemed acceptable)*. It made me sick. I was disturbed so much by those girls because… I also felt they robbed me of my happiness for a moment in time. Taking me back in time to reflect on my 300 lb days and all the years of hurt. I did realize that I had to work on this emotional trigger because there is going to be others in this world that I meet who will not know me as *"Carrie – 300 lbs"*.

Story Two: This was a weird but an first time experience and gave me a little insight as to what I might have to face with co-workers or other men moving forward.

One day about 11 months into my weight loss first year a male co-worker who had worked with me for 2 years and knew me pretty well as a obese woman. I was in a size 9 at the time and looking nice in my clothes. Very different than before. But there was no mystery and he was in the office during my weight loss period. I came in to work one day to pick up some papers and as I was leaving, he walks up to me and asks how I have been, what have been up to? Then hands me a business card with his cell phone number on the back and says call me sometime I would like to take you out to dinner.

Well I was in shock and taken aback for a minute. I stopped and thought for a minute… I had two split second feelings run through my head before I answered him… **one** *I resented the fact he waited until I was thin and acceptable before asking me out!* **two** *I was flattered and felt pretty!*

My response was said in a very sweet way… *"how come you waited until I lost weight to ask me out to dinner?"* and I smiled at him and pushed the door open and walked out. I felt really good as I left to get in my car. I handled it professionally while also getting my point across nicely. I will be honest with you when I say it did feel really good to turn him down. Only because it was a really good looking guy who knew me for 2 yrs 300 plus pounds and only after I lost the weight did he pull me aside and ask me out. I do not treat men this way nor do I feel this way anymore. But this was a first time experience.

<u>Story Three:</u> I was dating a guy about my 3rd year out and I don't really have a story per say but just something for everyone to think about and remember in case you start to feel this way.

We were doing something and I snapped at him saying *"who do you think you are, you didn't know me before I lost all the weight, you would have never even asked me out or talked to me when I was overweight"* I can't remember the circumstances around my words?

But what I had to work through and come to terms with is that I can't go around either blaming or judging people on whether they would or would not have spoken to me or asked me out in the past when I was obese. He did say to me he would hope that he was not that shallow of a person and would have still asked me out. but that he only knew me as how I was right then.

That's when I added another emotional challenge to the pile... something I had to deal with due to living half my life on one side of obesity and the other half my life not obese.

My significant other at the time of surgery was supportive and there for me in the beginning. But as I lost the weight he didn't even want to be seen with me in public and shut down on me. He would continually tell me I was too thin and I looked like a skeleton. This is not good for your self-worth or self-visual perspective at all. In fact I did start to feel depressed over it for a while. It wasn't until I went to a support group meeting and met with a few others, including my doctor, that I was told to try and communicate with him and ask if he would attend meetings with me and/or go into relationship counseling with me to get us through this. *"He said… he didn't have a problem and that it was all my fault, if I had not had the surgery, we would be fine."* Now I did go to counseling and this was a problem with his thoughts, but not my fault. This perspective on his part ultimately lead to me being depressed and hiding it and our separation and divorce. This is really important that you have your significant other truly involved and communicate all along the way.

Part of my reason for writing this book is to also help the significant others involved in your life understand and stick by you through the few years it takes to adjust to the new you. It all levels out in the end. But can be more challenging in so many more ways until then.

It is worth it!!

CHAPTER 8

New Experiences & Living Life "Different Choices"

It's strange but sometimes freedom can be in the form of losing the weight that keeps you fatigued, sluggish and imprisoned within your own body. Some people say *"You just have to put your mind to losing the weight"* well I found out that it is more complicated than that.

There are so many different factors involved. After a couple years post weight loss. I started thinking about and wanting to do all the activities and things that I was physically incapable of doing when at 300 lbs.

A girlfriend of mine I knew who had the microscopic gastric bypass surgery was one of my inspirations for thinking this way. She came into work one day and announced that she was resigning from her position to go and join the local police academy. I was in shock!

Before her weight loss... she worked two jobs, raising children in an abusive relationship with her husband. It was as if she was empowered to go after what she truly wanted to do. I haven't kept in contact with her to this day. but the last time I spoke to her a couple years after her announcement to join the police force, she was an officer, divorced and a single parent. She was happy and looked amazing.

I can't say that my post surgery life ended up moving in such a drastic change of careers. But it did change my life and there was a huge shift in direction. I did end up going to automotive tech school which I wouldn't have done when I was overweight. I also left the east coast and traveled by myself and my little dog to the south western side of the United States.

I am not sure how many other people change their lives in such dramatic ways? I truly believe it does open doors and allows a person to go after directions in life that you might not had considered before the weight loss.

I now enjoy my life with working on my cars, enjoy time with my little Shih Tzu dogs, and am physically capable of doing anything I want to in life

CHAPTER 9

Vitamins & Maintaining Healthy Eating Habits

Vitamins and healthy habits are one of the most challenging things to maintain over the rest of your life. At least it has been and I feel for myself it always will continue to be a challenge for life.

I tend to go through periods of time where I am in sync with my healthy life style and habits. Then there are times that I back slide and have to refocus on my health again. There doesn't seem to be any particular reason that triggers the back sliding times. At least not anything that I can pinpoint? Sometimes its financial costs of keeping up on the vitamins and protein shakes that I still do supplement with to this day.

Keeping the proper protein intake on a daily basis is challenging.

I don't feel I could do this without using the protein shakes. Also is finding chewable or liquid vitamins. There are a lot more products available today then there were in 2003.

I try and still drink two shakes daily, B12 chewable, and daily multivitamins chewable. I try and stay with as much chewable and liquid vitamins as possible. The stomach processing of food is different now and I want as much of what I take to be absorbed into my body as possible.

I continue to eat more meat, eggs and veggies and less carbohydrates to add to my protein levels. It has helped with my energy levels some.

If I were to pick out two of the most challenging things over the years for myself it would be:

1. *Healthy food selection when eating out or in a hurry.*

2. *Getting it through my head that I can't eat certain foods anymore.*

Healthy food selection when eating out or in a hurry? In the beginning it was the hardest thing to figure out. There was no road map for this and everyone who I spoke to said to either pack your own food or don't eat out. Well that is just not living in the real world with regards to work and family. Especially living in the Washington DC Metro area.

At first I had no choice but to pack my own food the first and into the second year. I did go through a harsh time the third and fourth years re-learning that I couldn't just eat anything out and ended up sick a lot!!

Then I started to think that if I am going to ever eat out again I had better pay attention to menus and places to eat that had a variety of food on their menu that I could order and eat. Also paying close attention to what foods your body rejects after the first two years post surgery is a good thing also, make a journal of foods that bother you so you can remember and keep up on it. Foods that may have bothered you or made you sick in the early years may not after a period of time.

I cannot still to this day eat rice or tuna fish at all without getting very sick. So if I order Chinese carryout I choose egg foo young and a combination of vegetable meals. Most places usually have chef salads. I can eat steak but it has to be cooked rare for me to be able to eat it. I also cannot eat chicken cooked on the grill or out to eat. It's usually to dry and will not stay down. If I cook the chicken breast myself I have learned how to cook it so that I am able to eat it, boiled. I can eat most all vegetables, salads, the meat listed above when cooked properly. I can also eat hamburgers on the grill and they have to be medium rare. Unless it is real meat then I am not able to keep it down. When I go out to eat now… I can find a meal on most all menus that I can eat for the most part.

Getting it through my head that I can't eat certain foods anymore? This was challenging… I remember one time about six weeks post surgery that I was out and decided to get an ice cream cone. Well about 5 to 10 min after I finished what I could eat at that time… I was walking through the video store and I just blacked out and fell straight back into my friends arms. It had to do with the sugar in take when my system was so cleaned out from that junk. I was warned by my doctor back then and you hear it from the support group meeting… but I ignored it and didn't believe them. (Haha) Yeah thick skull… I knew better! Yeah the learning curve on what I couldn't eat anymore was a steep one for me. I had to get sick and throw up a lot before learning this lesson. I would suggest for the first year and even maybe the second year to follow the doctors instructions or can get pretty painful.

It wasn't always me not listening to my doctor. Sometimes it was either I forgot and put it in my mouth and was quickly reminded that it was a bad idea or I had waited a period of time to go by and wanted to see if I could eat that food again in moderation. What I found to be true is that what you can and cannot eat does change over the years. So it may just be a matter of time till you can eat certain foods again or like with me some food has never came back into my life. Like rice and tuna are death to my stomach to this day.

Everyone is different and their bodies also. I would suggest small bites when trying to eat food you haven't eaten since the surgery. You will know within a few small bites of something whether or not you can eat it or not. I eat a few small bites then wait about 20 min to see if it is rejected or not by my stomach? This way I don't get sick as from eating too much too fast and regret it.

When your mom used to say as a child "chew your food slowly or slow down your eating to fast" This rule I feel truly applies to post surgery good eating habits.

CHAPTER 10

I Still Hate Exercise

I still am repulsed and bored with exercising... I have always found exercise just a chore to do. Since post surgery I have tried so many things to get into exercising on a regular basis. Wasted so much money on gym memberships, jazzercise, zumba, trainers and DVD collections to try and find something that I could finally stick to. Nothing...

The old faithful for me is power walking with an mp3 player. But again it's not in a consistent manor. I don't know what the solution is for someone who is like me and just doesn't have the passion for exercise? The gym and classes was either just boring, people staring at you, expense or finding time in the day to go, change into workout clothes, sweat and then go home or to work?

The DVD's would work for me if the trainer would slow down and teach you the proper moves and techniques to not cause injury before they went at warp speed in the workout. Also they tend to be too long and time consuming in order to complete a full workout. It's like 40 min for just abs, 40 min for just your core… bla, bla, bla!!

If I could design the perfect workout program for myself that I do feel I could stick to is a 30 min total body workout program. So for example:

1. *10 minute Full Body, Stretch workout.*

2. *30 minutes Full Body, Cardio workout.*

3. *30 minute Full Body, Toning workout. (with and without weights)*

4. *5 minute Full Body, Cool Down*

With a choice in various types of fun music selections.

I believe there is something out there for me that will keep my interest, be fun and not feel like it's a chore.

Tell me about your Journey, a friend, a relative or The Journey you are about to take?

Everyone has a story to tell. Everyone who is reading this book is in some stage of either being obese, losing weight, trying to lose weight or has already lost weight, is thin, or struggling to accept the person they see in the mirror. You and your loved ones are not alone and we all can benefit and grow from sharing the journey.

Include in your email the following things:

- **Your full name**
- **Your email address**
- **Your phone** *(if you want to be contacted to be in my next book)*
- **Your story / journey / experience / thoughts**
- **A picture of before and after** *(if you want to include)*
- **One or more things you are currently struggling with and would like to learn about alternatives help you through this time?**
- **Your acknowledgement that your story could be used in an upcoming book being put together now!**

SEND TO:

Carrie Litten

The Power of Thin

powerofthin@gmail.com or mypower@thepowerofthin.com

2001 E Lohman Avenue Suite 110, Las Cruces, NM 88001

ABOUT THE AUTHOR

Carrie Litten lives in Las Cruces, NM with three spoiled Shih Tzu dogs. She has a passion for classic cars, grilling out, friends and family. She believes in paying it forward and enjoying every minute that life has to offer.

Made in the USA
Middletown, DE
19 December 2014